SCHIRMER'S LIBRARY OF MUSICAL CLASSICS

Vol. 1590

WOLFGANG AMADEUS MOZART

Sinfonia Concertante

[K. 320d, formerly 364]

For Violin and Viola

The Orchestral Accompaniment

Transcribed for the Piano

ISBN 978-0-7935-5193-4

G. SCHIRMER, Inc.

DISTRIBUTED BY

HAL•LEONARD® CORPORATION

7777 W. BLUEMOUND RD. P.O. BOX 13819 MILWAUKEE, WI 53213

Printed in the U.S.A. by G. Schirmer, Inc.

Sinfonia Concertante

for Violin and Viola, with Orchestral Accompaniment

[K. 320ᵈ, formerly 364]

Wolfgang Amadeus Mozart

* This is an arrangement of the original accompaniment, which was for Strings, Oboes, and Horns in E. Orchestral material available on rental from the Publishers.

B

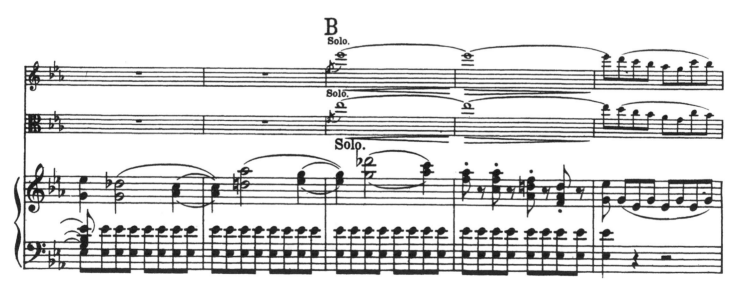

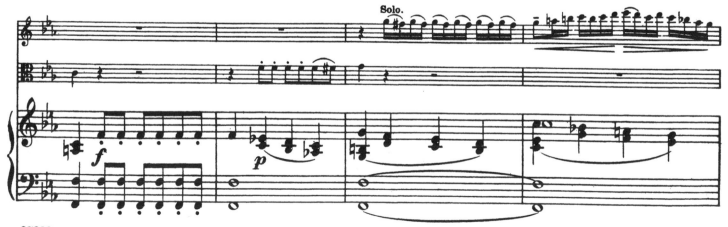

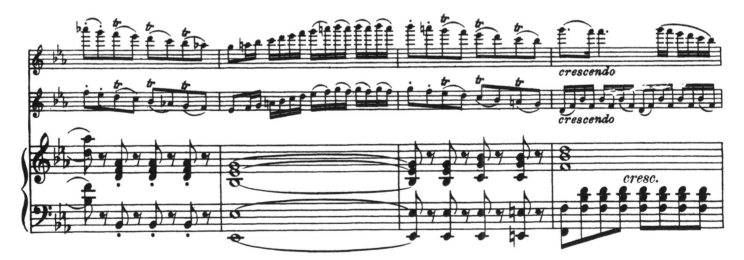

F

37888

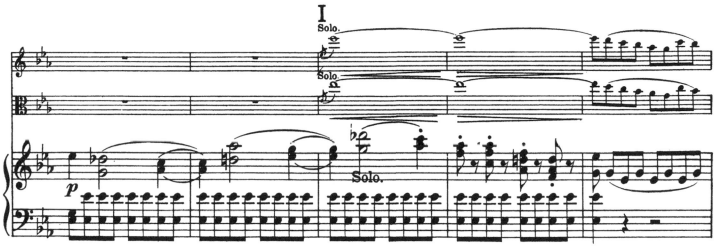

Solo.

Cadenza.

Adagio.

Andante.

Sinfonia Concertante

for Violin and Viola, with Orchestral Accompaniment

[K. 320ᵈ, formerly 364]

Violin

Wolfgang Amadeus Mozart

Printed in the U.S.A. by G. Schirmer, Inc.

Violin

3

Violin

Violin

Violin

Sinfonia Concertante

for Violin and Viola, with Orchestral Accompaniment

[K. 320ᵈ, formerly 364]

Viola

Wolfgang Amadeus Mozart

Printed in the U.S.A. by G. Schirmer, Inc.

Viola

Viola

Viola

Viola

8

Viola

PRESTO.

37883

Viola

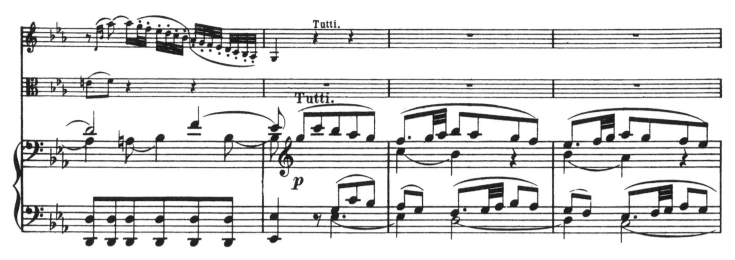

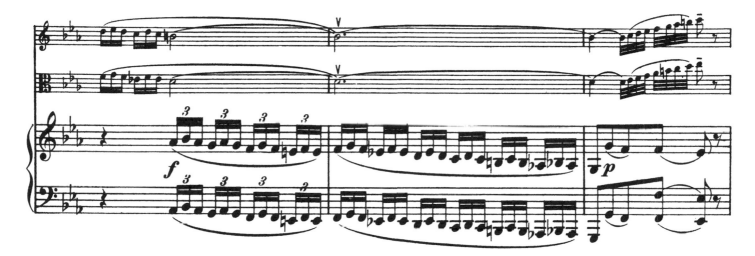

PRESTO.

37888

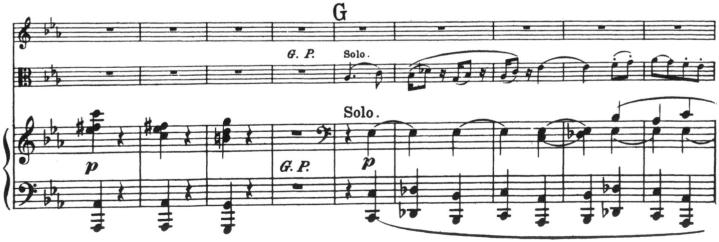

37883